As you begin to pay attention to your money and write down how you spend and what you spend money on, you will enter a new realm of possibilities. You do not have to make a lot of money to get a handle on your finances. These pages are for those people who are ready to see first-hand their spending habits and for those who are willing to adjust aspects of their spending habits. This will consequently bring about general life improvements.

It works when you write it down

If found, please contact and return to

Name: ______________________________

Phone: ______________________________

Email: ____________________

AF887471

Notes

EXPENSES		Mortgage/Rent				
		Groceries				
	Utilities	Electricity				
		Water				
		Cable				
		Phones				
	Transportation	Car Payment				
		Insurance				
		Lic/registration				
		Repairs				
	Family Care	Dad				
		Mom				
		Children				
		Miscellaneous				
Expenses Total						
INCOME		Paycheck				
		Tips/Bonuses				
		Other Income				
Income Total						
Surplus/Deficit						

Notes

EXPENSES		Mortgage/Rent				
		Groceries				
	Utilities	Electricity				
		Water				
		Cable				
		Phones				
	Transportation	Car Payment				
		Insurance				
		Lic/registration				
		Repairs				
	Family Care	Dad				
		Mom				
		Children				
		Miscellaneous				
Expenses Total						
INCOME		Paycheck				
		Tips/Bonuses				
		Other Income				
Income Total						
Surplus/Deficit						

Notes

EXPENSES		Mortgage/Rent				
		Groceries				
	Utilities	Electricity				
		Water				
		Cable				
		Phones				
	Transportation	Car Payment				
		Insurance				
		Lic/registration				
		Repairs				
	Family Care	Dad				
		Mom				
		Children				
		Miscellaneous				
Expenses Total						
INCOME		Paycheck				
		Tips/Bonuses				
		Other Income				
Income Total						
Surplus/Deficit						

Notes

EXPENSES		Mortgage/Rent				
		Groceries				
	Utilities	Electricity				
		Water				
		Cable				
		Phones				
	Transportation	Car Payment				
		Insurance				
		Lic/registration				
		Repairs				
	Family Care	Dad				
		Mom				
		Children				
		Miscellaneous				
Expenses Total						
INCOME		Paycheck				
		Tips/Bonuses				
		Other Income				
Income Total						
Surplus/Deficit						

Notes

EXPENSES		Mortgage/Rent				
		Groceries				
	Utilities	Electricity				
		Water				
		Cable				
		Phones				
	Transportation	Car Payment				
		Insurance				
		Lic/registration				
		Repairs				
	Family Care	Dad				
		Mom				
		Children				
		Miscellaneous				
Expenses Total						
INCOME		Paycheck				
		Tips/Bonuses				
		Other Income				
Income Total						
Surplus/Deficit						

Notes

EXPENSES		Mortgage/Rent				
		Groceries				
	Utilities	Electricity				
		Water				
		Cable				
		Phones				
	Transportation	Car Payment				
		Insurance				
		Lic/registration				
		Repairs				
	Family Care	Dad				
		Mom				
		Children				
		Miscellaneous				
Expenses Total						
INCOME		Paycheck				
		Tips/Bonuses				
		Other Income				
Income Total						
Surplus/Deficit						

Notes

EXPENSES		Mortgage/Rent				
		Groceries				
	Utilities	Electricity				
		Water				
		Cable				
		Phones				
	Transportation	Car Payment				
		Insurance				
		Lic/registration				
		Repairs				
	Family Care	Dad				
		Mom				
		Children				
		Miscellaneous				
Expenses Total						
INCOME		Paycheck				
		Tips/Bonuses				
		Other Income				
Income Total						
Surplus/Deficit						

Notes

EXPENSES		Mortgage/Rent				
		Groceries				
	Utilities	Electricity				
		Water				
		Cable				
		Phones				
	Transportation	Car Payment				
		Insurance				
		Lic/registration				
		Repairs				
	Family Care	Dad				
		Mom				
		Children				
		Miscellaneous				
Expenses Total						
INCOME		Paycheck				
		Tips/Bonuses				
		Other Income				
Income Total						
Surplus/Deficit						

Notes

EXPENSES		Mortgage/Rent				
		Groceries				
	Utilities	Electricity				
		Water				
		Cable				
		Phones				
	Transportation	Car Payment				
		Insurance				
		Lic/registration				
		Repairs				
	Family Care	Dad				
		Mom				
		Children				
		Miscellaneous				
Expenses Total						
INCOME		Paycheck				
		Tips/Bonuses				
		Other Income				
Income Total						
Surplus/Deficit						

Notes

EXPENSES		Mortgage/Rent				
		Groceries				
	Utilities	Electricity				
		Water				
		Cable				
		Phones				
	Transportation	Car Payment				
		Insurance				
		Lic/registration				
		Repairs				
	Family Care	Dad				
		Mom				
		Children				
		Miscellaneous				
Expenses Total						
INCOME		Paycheck				
		Tips/Bonuses				
		Other Income				
Income Total						
Surplus/Deficit						

Notes

EXPENSES		Mortgage/Rent				
		Groceries				
	Utilities	Electricity				
		Water				
		Cable				
		Phones				
	Transportation	Car Payment				
		Insurance				
		Lic/registration				
		Repairs				
	Family Care	Dad				
		Mom				
		Children				
		Miscellaneous				
		Expenses Total				
INCOME		Paycheck				
		Tips/Bonuses				
		Other Income				
		Income Total				
Surplus/Deficit						

Notes

EXPENSES		Mortgage/Rent				
		Groceries				
	Utilities	Electricity				
		Water				
		Cable				
		Phones				
	Transportation	Car Payment				
		Insurance				
		Lic/registration				
		Repairs				
	Family Care	Dad				
		Mom				
		Children				
		Miscellaneous				
Expenses Total						
INCOME		Paycheck				
		Tips/Bonuses				
		Other Income				
Income Total						
Surplus/Deficit						

Notes

EXPENSES		Mortgage/Rent				
		Groceries				
	Utilities	Electricity				
		Water				
		Cable				
		Phones				
	Transportation	Car Payment				
		Insurance				
		Lic/registration				
		Repairs				
	Family Care	Dad				
		Mom				
		Children				
		Miscellaneous				
		Expenses Total				
INCOME		Paycheck				
		Tips/Bonuses				
		Other Income				
		Income Total				
		Surplus/Deficit				

Notes

EXPENSES		Mortgage/Rent				
		Groceries				
	Utilities	Electricity				
		Water				
		Cable				
		Phones				
	Transportation	Car Payment				
		Insurance				
		Lic/registration				
		Repairs				
	Family Care	Dad				
		Mom				
		Children				
		Miscellaneous				
Expenses Total						
INCOME		Paycheck				
		Tips/Bonuses				
		Other Income				
Income Total						
Surplus/Deficit						

Notes

EXPENSES		Mortgage/Rent				
		Groceries				
	Utilities	Electricity				
		Water				
		Cable				
		Phones				
	Transportation	Car Payment				
		Insurance				
		Lic/registration				
		Repairs				
	Family Care	Dad				
		Mom				
		Children				
		Miscellaneous				
Expenses Total						
INCOME		Paycheck				
		Tips/Bonuses				
		Other Income				
Income Total						
Surplus/Deficit						

Notes

EXPENSES		Mortgage/Rent				
		Groceries				
	Utilities	Electricity				
		Water				
		Cable				
		Phones				
	Transportation	Car Payment				
		Insurance				
		Lic/registration				
		Repairs				
	Family Care	Dad				
		Mom				
		Children				
		Miscellaneous				
Expenses Total						
INCOME		Paycheck				
		Tips/Bonuses				
		Other Income				
Income Total						
Surplus/Deficit						

Notes

EXPENSES	Mortgage/Rent					
	Groceries					
	Utilities	Electricity				
		Water				
		Cable				
		Phones				
	Transportation	Car Payment				
		Insurance				
		Lic/registration				
		Repairs				
	Family Care	Dad				
		Mom				
		Children				
	Miscellaneous					
Expenses Total						
INCOME	Paycheck					
	Tips/Bonuses					
	Other Income					
Income Total						
Surplus/Deficit						

Notes

EXPENSES		Mortgage/Rent				
		Groceries				
	Utilities	Electricity				
		Water				
		Cable				
		Phones				
	Transportation	Car Payment				
		Insurance				
		Lic/registration				
		Repairs				
	Family Care	Dad				
		Mom				
		Children				
		Miscellaneous				
Expenses Total						
INCOME		Paycheck				
		Tips/Bonuses				
		Other Income				
Income Total						
Surplus/Deficit						

Made in the USA
Coppell, TX
04 November 2026

11287995R00022